For those who have learned to survive.

And for those now learning to receive.

For the ones who have carried too much alone, for too long, and are finally allowing themselves to be watered.

For the people who remind us that God often nourishes us through others, through love, through presence, and through mercy we didn't think we deserved.

May this season teach you that being supported is not weakness.

It's part of the healing process.

Healing isn't only what you eat.

It's what you receive.

It's what you allow.

It's what you finally stop resisting.

— Jackie

"He makes me lie down in green pastures. He leads me beside quiet waters, he refreshes my soul."
— *Psalm 23:2–3 (NIV)*

Foreword

When I wrote *The Internal Fungus Among Us*, I thought healing would feel like an ending.

I thought it would be the moment everything finally started mending, the moment my body calmed down, when I could exhale and return to normal life.

But healing rarely works like that.

What I learned is that healing is not just recovery. It is rebuilding. It is learning how to live again after survival and learning how to trust yourself after your body has carried you through seasons you never thought you'd endure.

After years of navigating gut dysfunction, inflammation, exhaustion, and mystery symptoms, I began to find answers. I began to feel stronger. I began to experience clarity. But even then, the deeper work remained.

The deeper work was learning how to *receive*.

Because survival teaches you to do everything alone. Survival teaches you to push through. Survival teaches you to become independent out of necessity.

But healing invites a whole new lesson.

Healing asks you to slow down. To settle in. To soften.

Healing asks you to let yourself be watered.

Sometimes that watering comes through food, hydration, rest, and gentle routines.

Other times it comes through relationships, support, prayer, and love.

And sometimes, it comes through moments you did not plan for, moments that interrupt your life and remind you that you cannot always do everything on your own.

That was true for me again after unexpected setbacks, physical challenges, and moments that forced me to slow down. These became parts of another chapter in the same message God has been teaching me all along.

You are not meant to heal alone.

I created *Watered & Whole* as your companion for this season, a season in which your healing becomes less about force and more about nourishment. Less about fixing and more about receiving.

Over the next ninety days, you will be invited to nourish your body, calm your mind, and tend to your spirit through Scripture, reflection, and whole-body practices that restore you from the inside out.

Some days will feel peaceful. Some days will feel emotional. Some days you may not know what to write at all.

Feel proud for showing up.

Preface

Rooted in Scripture and designed to support faith-centered healing of the mind, body, and spirit.

Healing is not only about what we remove.

It is also about what we restore.

If *Rooted & Renewed* was about grounding and rebuilding your foundation, *Watered & Whole* is about what happens next— when the soil is ready and the roots are eager to receive.

This devotional journal was created for the woman who is tired of surviving.

For the one who has been strong for everyone else.

For the one who has done the hard work, prayed the prayers, pushed through the pain, and kept going even when no one understood what she was carrying.

Now it is time to be nourished. Not only through food and hydration, but through rest, gentleness, love, connection, and spiritual renewal.

This season is about learning to soften, learning to trust again, and learning to let the body and heart receive what they have been deprived of for too long.

My prayer is that this journal becomes a safe space for you.

Acknowledgments

Much gratitude to everyone who has fed me spiritually or physically and walked alongside me on this healing journey. Your support was the soil in which my work thrived and grew.

Thank you—

To the friends, readers, and mentors who shared their stories and life experiences. You reminded me that healing is possible.

To my family, my tribe, for reminding me of what it feels like to come back to myself. You are loving, funny, patient, and grounding in all the ways that matter most.

To the teachers, practitioners, faith organizations, and study groups who continue to inspire and motivate my work, for planting seeds of wisdom that keep growing long after the conversation ends.

To Andrea Baugher, for your thoughtful editing eye, steady consistency, and devotion to excellence. This book is stronger because of you.

To V. Rowan, your illustrations and quiet support matter.

And most importantly, to God—the ultimate healer, teacher, and restorer of peace.

Every page is an offering of gratitude for the quiet miracles that happen when we finally slow down and listen.

How to Use This Journal

Healing is not a one-time moment.

It is a rhythm you return to, one breath, one prayer, and one small act of nourishment at a time.

Every day is an invitation to slow down, listen to your body, and reconnect with God's presence in your healing process.

This 90-day devotional journal was created to help you step into a season of receiving, where nourishment becomes your practice and wholeness becomes your new way of living.

Here's how to begin:

1. Make a sacred space.

Choose a quiet time and place, morning or evening, where you can sit with your journal for 10 minutes. Bring your Bible, a pen, and a gentle heart.

2. Read the Scripture slowly.

Let the verse speak to you. Circle words that stand out. Write them again if they bring peace.

3. Reflect with intention.

Use the prompt to explore how the passage applies to your healing—physically, emotionally, and spiritually.

4. Write what is true for you.

There is no "right" method of journaling. Simply acknowledge the reality of this season, this moment—whatever it is. Some days you'll fill the page. Some days you'll have only a single sentence. Both are enough, as long as you're being honest.

5. Close with gratitude or prayer.

Let your final thought be one of release. Thank God for what is unfolding, even if it is still in progress.

This journal is arranged in three parts, each guiding you through thirty days of healing focus:

Days 1–30: Replenish & Receive

"Come, all you who are thirsty, come to the waters..."
— *Isaiah 55:1 (NIV)*

This first section is about nourishment at the foundation level. Hydration, rest, replenishment, and learning to receive support without guilt. Here you begin to soften and allow yourself to be cared for.

Days 31–60: Open & Overflow

"Above all, love each other deeply..."
— *1 Peter 4:8 (NIV)*

This second section is about emotional nourishment. Healing through connection, boundaries, compassion, forgiveness, and love without depletion. Here you begin to open your heart and trust what God is restoring within you.

Days 61–90: Thrive & Trust

"And the God of all grace...will himself restore you and make you strong."
— *1 Peter 5:10 (NIV)*

This final section is about embodied wholeness. Confidence in your healing, strength in your identity, trust in your relationships, and joy in the life you are rebuilding. Here you begin to thrive and trust the season you are stepping into.

After ninety days, this practice becomes more than journaling. It becomes a way of living.

Begin where you are. Let the pages hold you gently. And remember, healing is not only what you do.

It is what you allow.

Let's begin.

Part 1: Replenish & Receive (Days 1–30)

"Come, all you who are thirsty, come to the waters..."
— *Isaiah 55:1 (NIV)*

This season is not about striving.

It is about softening.

It is about letting your body exhale and allowing nourishment to reach places that have been depleted for too long.

Here, you are invited to replenish through hydration, rest, nourishment, and the quiet courage of receiving support.

You do not have to do everything alone.

You are allowed to be watered.

* * *

Day 1: Watered by Prayer

Scripture:

"He leads me beside quiet waters, he refreshes my soul."
— *Psalm 23:2–3 (NIV)*

* * *

Affirmation:

I allow myself to be refreshed by prayer, not effort.

Reflection Prompt:

Where in your life are you being invited to stop striving and simply receive?

Journal Space:

Reflect & Respond

[1]

---

[1] Take a slow sip of water. Remember that God restores gently.

Day 2: Nourishment Without Guilt

Scripture:

"Therefore I tell you, do not worry about your life, what you will eat or drink..."
— *Matthew 6:25 (NIV)*

* * *

Affirmation:

I nourish my body without guilt. I am worthy of care.

Reflection Prompt:

Do you ever feel guilt for resting, eating well, or receiving support? Where did that belief begin?

Journal Space:

Reflect & Respond

[2]

---

[2] Today, choose one small nourishing thing and let it be enough.

Day 3: Let Yourself Be Held

Scripture:

"Cast all your anxiety on him because he cares for you."
— *1 Peter 5:7 (NIV)*

* * *

Affirmation:

I release what I cannot carry. I am held.

Reflection Prompt:

What are you still trying to carry alone that God is asking you to release?

Journal Space:

Reflect & Respond

[3]

---

[3] If your body feels heavy today, pause and take three slow breaths before moving on.

Day 4: Receiving Is Healing

Scripture:

"Ask and it will be given to you; seek and you will find..."
— *Matthew 7:7 (NIV)*

* * *

Affirmation:

I am learning to receive with humility and trust.

Reflection Prompt:

Which feels hardest for you to receive: help, love, compliments, time, or care?

Journal Space:

Reflect & Respond

4

---

[4] Let someone do something kind for you today, without explaining or apologizing to them.

Day 5: Hydration as Devotion

Scripture:

"Whoever drinks the water I give them will never thirst."
— *John 4:14 (NIV)*

* * *

Affirmation:

I nourish my body with what it truly needs.

Reflection Prompt:

How could hydration, nourishment, or daily care become a spiritual act instead of a task?

Journal Space:

Reflect & Respond

[5]

---

[5] If you can, make one meal or snack today slower and more mindful.

Day 6: Gentle Strength

Scripture:

"My grace is sufficient for you, for my power is made perfect in weakness."
— *2 Corinthians 12:9 (NIV)*

* * *

Affirmation:

I am strong even when I soften.

Reflection Prompt:

When in your life have you confused strength with pushing? What would strength look like if it were gentle?

Journal Space:

Reflect & Respond

⁶

---

⁶ If you feel tension today, place your hand on your heart and whisper, "I am safe to soften."

Day 7: Rest as Replenishment

Scripture:

"In peace I will lie down and sleep, for you alone, Lord, make me dwell in safety."
— *Psalm 4:8 (NIV)*

* * *

Affirmation:

My rest restores me. I am safe to slow down.

Reflection Prompt:

What does your body need most right now: sleep, stillness, softness, nourishment, or reassurance?

Journal Space:

Reflect & Respond

7

---

[7] Tonight, consider dimming the lights early and letting your body unwind without guilt.

Week 1 Reflection: The Courage to Receive

Scripture:

"Come to me, all you who are weary and burdened, and I will give you rest."
— *Matthew 11:28 (NIV)*

* * *

Affirmation:

I am learning that receiving is not weakness. It is healing.

Reflection Prompts:

This first week invited you into a different kind of strength. Not the strength of pushing through, but the strength of letting yourself be cared for.

Take a few quiet minutes to reflect:

1. Where did you feel resistance to slowing down this week?
2. Which moment felt most nourishing physically, emotionally, or spiritually?
3. What did your body respond to with gratitude?
4. Where did you notice God meeting you gently?
5. What is one way you can receive more support in the week ahead?

Reflect & Respond

Day 8: Gentle Hydration

Scripture:

"Whoever believes in me, as Scripture has said, rivers of living water will flow from within them."
— *John 7:38 (NIV)*

* * *

Affirmation:

Life flows through me with ease. I am replenished.

Reflection Prompt:

Where in your body or life do you feel dry, depleted, or in need of renewal?

Journal Space:

Reflect & Respond

---

[8] Drink water today as a simple act of devotion, not discipline.

Day 9: A Softer Pace

Scripture:

"Be still, and know that I am God."
— *Psalm 46:10 (NIV)*

* * *

Affirmation:

I am allowed to slow down. Stillness restores me.

Reflection Prompt:

What would change if you moved through today with less urgency?

Journal Space:

Reflect & Respond

[9]

Day 10: Safe to Receive

Scripture:

"Every good and perfect gift is from above..."
—*James 1:17 (NIV)*

* * *

Affirmation:

I am safe to receive goodness.

Reflection Prompt:

What is one good thing in your life that you struggle to fully accept or enjoy?
What is one small shift you can make to get closer to full acceptance and enjoyment?

Journal Space:

Reflect & Respond

[10]

---

[10] Let yourself enjoy something small today without rushing through it.

Day 11: Nourishment in the Present

Scripture:

"Rejoice always, pray continually, give thanks in all circumstances..."
— *1 Thessalonians 5:16–18 (NIV)*

* * *

Affirmation:

I nourish myself by staying present.

Reflection Prompt:

Where does your mind tend to go when you are not fully present? How does that affect your body?

Journal Space:

Reflect & Respond

[11]

---

[11] Choose one moment today to be fully present, with no multitasking.

Day 12: Rest Without Explanation

Scripture:

"In repentance and rest is your salvation, in quietness and trust is your strength."
— *Isaiah 30:15 (NIV)*

* * *

Affirmation:

I rest without guilt. My body heals in quietness.

Reflection Prompt:

Which part of you feels like it needs permission to rest?

Journal Space:

Reflect & Respond

---

[12] Rest is not laziness; it is repair.

Day 13: Replenished in Love

Scripture:

"We love because he first loved us."
— *1 John 4:19 (NIV)*

* * *

Affirmation:

I am nourished by love that is steady and safe.

Reflection Prompt:

Where have you been seeking love through effort instead of receiving it naturally?

Journal Space:

Reflect & Respond

13

---

[13] If you feel lonely today, place your hand on your heart and remember: you are already loved.

Day 14: The Gift of Gentle Care

Scripture:

"He tends his flock like a shepherd: He gathers the lambs in his arms and carries them close to his heart."
— *Isaiah 40:11 (NIV)*

* * *

Affirmation:

I am cared for. I am carried. I am not alone.

Reflection Prompt:

Knowing God is carrying you close today, which burden can you stop holding so tightly?

Journal Space:

Reflect & Respond

[14]

---

[14] Do one nurturing thing today that feels like comfort, not productivity.

Week 2 Reflection: Replenish & Receive

Scripture:

"I will be fully satisfied as with the richest of foods; with singing lips my mouth will praise you."
— *Psalm 63:5 (NIV)*

* * *

Affirmation:

I am learning to receive what nourishes me, without guilt or resistance.

Reflection Prompts:

This week invited you to slow down and notice what replenishes you. You practiced receiving instead of striving, allowing rest to become healing, and letting love feel safe again.

Take a few quiet minutes to reflect:

1. Where did you feel most replenished this week?
2. Where in your body did you feel the most at ease or stressed out?
3. Where did you notice yourself resisting rest, support, or nourishment?
4. What would it look like to nourish yourself even more intentionally in the days ahead?
5. What did you receive this week that surprised you?

Reflect & Respond

Day 15: Hydration and Healing

Scripture:

"Whoever believes in me, as Scripture has said, rivers of living water will flow from within them."
— *John 7:38 (NIV)*

* * *

Affirmation:

Life flows through me. I am hydrated, replenished, and restored.

Reflection Prompt:

Where in your life are you ready to allow more flow instead of holding everything in or trying to maintain control?

Journal Space:

Reflect & Respond

---

[15] If you can, add a pinch of mineral salt or lemon to your water today for gentle support.

Day 16: Nourishment Through Rest

Scripture:

"In peace I will lie down and sleep, for you alone, Lord, make me dwell in safety."
— *Psalm 4:8 (NIV)*

* * *

Affirmation:

Rest is safe for me. My body restores itself naturally.

Reflection Prompt:

What prevents you from getting enough rest?
What might your body need from you tonight?

Journal Space:

Reflect & Respond

[16]

---

[16] Tonight, consider turning your phone off 30 minutes earlier than usual.

Day 17: Receiving Calm

Scripture:

"You will keep in perfect peace those whose minds are steadfast, because they trust in you."
— *Isaiah 26:3 (NIV)*

* * *

Affirmation:

Peace is available to me. I choose calm.

Reflection Prompt:

What thought pattern pulls you away from peace most often? What would it feel like to release it?

Journal Space:

Reflect & Respond

[17]

---

[17] Try breathing in slowly for 4 counts and out for 6 counts, just once today.

Day 18: Digesting Life Slowly

Scripture:

"Pleasant words are a honeycomb, sweet to the soul and healing to the bones."
— *Proverbs 16:24 (NIV)*

* * *

Affirmation:

I speak kindly to myself. My body responds to gentleness.

Reflection Prompt:

What emotional "food" have you been consuming lately that nourishes you?
What have you been consuming that drains you instead?

Journal Space:

Reflect & Respond

¹⁸

---

¹⁸ Today, notice the words you speak to yourself, and choose softer ones on purpose.

Day 19: Comforted and Cared For

Scripture:

"As a mother comforts her child, so will I comfort you."
— *Isaiah 66:13 (NIV)*

* * *

Affirmation:

I am comforted. I am cared for. I allow myself to receive love.

Reflection Prompt:

What does comfort feel like in your body?
What do you need more of right now?

Journal Space:

Reflect & Respond

---

[19] Wrap yourself in warmth today—a blanket, a sweatshirt, or a quiet moment that feels safe.

Day 20: Nourished by Gratitude

Scripture:

"Give thanks in all circumstances; for this is God's will for you in Christ Jesus."
— *1 Thessalonians 5:18 (NIV)*

* * *

Affirmation:

Gratitude nourishes me from the inside out.

Reflection Prompt:

List three things your body has done for you recently that deserve appreciation.

Journal Space:

Reflect & Respond

20

---

[20] Before eating today, pause for ten seconds and offer quiet gratitude.

Day 21: Love That Restores

Scripture:

"Above all, love each other deeply, because love covers over a multitude of sins."
— *1 Peter 4:8 (NIV)*

* * *

Affirmation:

I am open to love that restores, not love that drains.

Reflection Prompt:

What does healthy love look like for you right now?
What kind of love are you no longer willing to accept?

Journal Space:

Reflect & Respond

[21]

---

[21] Today, ask yourself, "Does this relationship nourish me or deplete me?"

Week 3 Reflection: Nourishment & Discernment

Scripture:

"You have searched me, Lord, and you know me."
— *Psalm 139:1 (NIV)*

* * *

Affirmation:

I am learning what nourishes me, and I am releasing what drains me.

Reflection Prompts:

This week invited you to reflect on nourishment in a deeper way. Not just nourishment through food, hydration, and rest, but nourishment through emotions, relationships, and the way you care for your inner world.

As you slowed down, you may have noticed what restores you and what quietly depletes you. Take a few moments to reflect:

1. What brought you comfort this week?
2. What did you consume, mentally or emotionally, that felt nourishing, and what felt draining?
3. Where did you notice yourself giving too much of your energy away?
4. Which relationship, routine, or habit felt most supportive to your healing?

Reflect & Respond

Day 22: Nourished by Faith, Not Fear

Scripture:

"When I am afraid, I put my trust in you."
— *Psalm 56:3 (NIV)*

* * *

Affirmation:

I choose faith over fear. My body responds to trust.

Reflection Prompt:

What fear has been draining your peace lately?
What would it look like to surrender that fear to God today?

Journal Space:

Reflect & Respond

---

[22] When fear rises, place your hand on your chest and whisper a prayer: "I trust You."

Day 23: Healing Through Nourishing Connection

Scripture:

"Carry each other's burdens, and in this way you will fulfill the law of Christ."
— *Galatians 6:2 (NIV)*

* * *

Affirmation:

I allow connection to support my healing.

Reflection Prompt:

Who helps you feel safe, seen, or supported?
Where might God be inviting you to stop isolating and let someone in?

Journal Space:

Reflect & Respond

[23]

---

[23] Send one message today, not to perform but to connect.

Day 24: Nourished by Truth

Scripture:

"Then you will know the truth, and the truth will set you free."
— *John 8:32 (NIV)*

* * *

Affirmation:

Truth nourishes me. Clarity restores me.

Reflection Prompt:

What truth about your body, healing, or life are you avoiding?
What freedom might come if you faced it gently and honestly?

Journal Space:

Reflect & Respond

Day 25: Releasing What Depletes You

Scripture:

"Come to me, all you who are weary and burdened, and I will give you rest."
— *Matthew 11:28 (NIV)*

* * *

Affirmation:

I release what drains me. I welcome what restores me.

Reflection Prompt:

What has been quietly draining your energy lately?
What is one boundary you could set that would protect your peace?

Journal Space:

Reflect & Respond

[25]

---

[25] Sometimes nourishment begins with removing what exhausts you.

Day 26: Love That Feels Safe

Scripture:

"[Love] always protects, always trusts, always hopes, always perseveres."
— *1 Corinthians 13:7 (NIV)*

* * *

Affirmation:

I am open to love that feels safe, steady, and peaceful.

Reflection Prompt:

What does safe love feel like in your body?
When in the past have you confused intensity with love?

Journal Space:

Reflect & Respond

26

Day 27: Replenished Through Simplicity

Scripture:

"But godliness with contentment is great gain."
— *1 Timothy 6:6 (NIV)*

* * *

Affirmation:

Simplicity restores me. Peace is enough.

Reflection Prompt:

Which aspects of your life feel too complicated right now? What could you simplify so your mind can rest and your body can relax?

Journal Space:

Reflect & Respond

---

[27] Consider ridding yourself of a physical item or internal belief that you no longer need.

Day 28: Gratitude That Grounds You

Scripture:

"Rooted and built up in him...overflowing with thankfulness."
— *Colossians 2:7 (NIV)*

* * *

Affirmation:

Gratitude strengthens me. I am grounded in appreciation.

Reflection Prompt:

What are three things you are grateful for right now, even in the middle of healing?

Journal Space:

Reflect & Respond

[28]

---

[28] Gratitude is not denial; it is nourishment.

Week 4 Reflection: Replenished in Peace

Scripture:

"He refreshes my soul."
— *Psalm 23:3 (NIV)*

* * *

Affirmation:

I am replenished in peace. I am learning to receive what restores me.

Reflection Prompts:

This week invited you to continue softening into nourishment. You practiced listening to what your body needs, recognizing what drains your energy, and allowing yourself to receive care without guilt.

Healing does not always happen through big changes. Often it happens through small choices repeated with love.

Take a few quiet minutes to reflect:

1. Where in your heart, mind, or body have you noticed yourself becoming more replenished or restored?
2. Which habit, practice, or mindset has supported your healing the most this month?
3. What has been draining you that you are now ready to release?
4. Where do you still feel resistance to receiving love, rest, or support?

Reflect & Respond

Day 29: Receiving Without Fear

Scripture:

"Do not be anxious about anything, but in every situation, by prayer and petition, with thanksgiving, present your requests to God."
— *Philippians 4:6 (NIV)*

* * *

Affirmation:

I am safe to ask. I am safe to receive.

Reflection Prompt:

What do you need right now that you have been afraid to ask for? If you fully trusted God's care, what would you allow yourself to receive?

Journal Space:

Reflect & Respond

---

[29] Today, practice receiving, even if it is something small like help, kindness, or reassurance.

Day 30: Replenished and Whole

Scripture:

"May the God of hope fill you with all joy and peace as you trust in him..."
— *Romans 15:13 (NIV)*

* * *

Affirmation:

I am replenished. I am supported. I am becoming whole.

Reflection Prompt:

What has shifted in you over the past thirty days, even subtly? What do you want to carry forward into the next season of healing?

Journal Space:

Reflect & Respond

[30]

---

[30] Pause today and honor your progress. Growth counts, even when it is quiet.

Pause & Pray: Replenished

Take a slow breath.
Let your shoulders soften.
Let your body settle.
Embrace that you have spent the last thirty days practicing
something holy and meaningful.

Prayer:

God,
Thank you for meeting me in the quiet.
Thank you for restoring what has been tired in me.

Thank you for the nourishment I have received,
through rest, through breath, through stillness,
and through the gentle reminders that I am not alone.

Guide me to continue releasing the belief that I have to carry
everything myself.

Teach me to listen to my body with compassion.

And moving forward, help me remain open,
not hardened by what I have survived
but softened by what you are rebuilding within me.

Water what is still dry.
Strengthen what is still weak.
And remind me daily that peace is available to me.

Amen.

Part 2: Open & Overflow (Days 31–60)

"Above all, love each other deeply, because love covers over a multitude of sins."
— *1 Peter 4:8 (NIV)*

Now it is time to open.

This section focuses on emotional nourishment, healing through connection, and learning how to love without losing yourself.

You will explore forgiveness, boundaries, compassion, and the courage it takes to soften after survival.

Some pages may feel painful. Some may feel freeing.

But all of it is part of becoming the whole you.

Let this season remind you that healing is not only physical.

It is relational.

And love, when it is rooted in God, is meant to overflow.

* * *

Day 31: Open the Heart Gently

Scripture:

"Above all else, guard your heart, for everything you do flows from it."
— *Proverbs 4:23 (NIV)*

* * *

Affirmation:

I open my heart with wisdom. I protect my peace with love.

Reflection Prompt:

Is it easy or challenging to give others access to your heart? Explore times in your past that may have become obstacles to doing this now.
What would it look like to open your heart gently without abandoning yourself?

Journal Space:

Reflect & Respond

[31]

---

[31] Consider listening to the song "Open the Eyes of My Heart" by Paul Baloche—and sing praises to Him.

Day 32: Love Without Depletion

Scripture:

"Love is patient, love is kind..."
— *1 Corinthians 13:4 (NIV)*

* * *

Affirmation:

I give love freely, and I do not give myself away.

Reflection Prompt:

Where have you been over-giving in the name of love?
What boundary would allow love to stay healthy instead of
exhausting?

Journal Page:

Reflect & Respond

32

---

[32] If you feel drained today, pause and ask, "What do I need right now?" Consider taking a step toward healing.

Day 33: Healing Through Forgiveness

Scripture:

"Be kind and compassionate to one another, forgiving each other..."
— *Ephesians 4:32 (NIV)*

* * *

Affirmation:

Forgiveness frees my heart. I release what I no longer want to carry.

Reflection Prompt:

Toward whom or what are you holding resentment?
What would it feel like to release that weight, even if it is slowly?

Journal Space:

Reflect & Respond

³³

---

[33] Forgiveness does not excuse the past; it frees your body from carrying it.

Day 34: Receiving Love

Scripture:

"We love because he first loved us."
— *1 John 4:19 (NIV)*

* * *

Affirmation:

I am worthy of love that is steady, safe, and sincere.

Reflection Prompt:

Do you allow yourself to receive love easily, or do you resist it? What fear rises in you when love feels real and safe?

Journal Space:

Reflect & Respond

---

[34] Let yourself receive a compliment today without deflecting it.

Day 35: God Heals the Heart

Scripture:

"He heals the brokenhearted and binds up their wounds."
— *Psalm 147:3 (NIV)*

* * *

Affirmation:

God is healing what I cannot fix. My heart is safe in His hands.

Reflection Prompt:

What part of your heart still feels wounded or tired?
What would you ask God to heal in you if you could be
completely honest?

Journal Space:

Reflect & Respond

[35]

---

[35] Today, speak gently to yourself the way you would speak to someone you love.

Week 5 Reflection: Opening the Heart

Scripture:

"The Lord is my strength and my shield; in him my heart trusts, and I am helped; my heart exults, and with my song I give thanks to him."
— *Psalm 28:7 (NIV)*

* * *

Affirmation:

I'm learning to recognize where I've been closed off. I'm opening my heart with gentleness and compassion as I heal.

Reflection Prompts:

This week invited you to soften your heart toward God and others, opening yourself to love, joy, and freedom while leaving room for helpful boundaries.

By practicing release and forgiveness, you freed yourself to heal and receive.

1. How did your body respond to allowing yourself to soften?
2. How did you face the fears that come with releasing resentment?
3. What did you notice when you chose openness instead of protection?
4. How will you continue to stay open while honoring your boundaries in the coming week?

Reflect & Respond

Day 36: Boundaries Are Love

Scripture:

"Let your 'Yes' be yes, and your 'No,' no."
— *Matthew 5:37 (NIV)*

* * *

Affirmation:

I honor my limits. Boundaries protect what is sacred.

Reflection Prompt:

Where do you need a stronger "no" in your life?
What would change if you believed that boundaries are an act of love?

Journal Space:

Reflect & Respond

[36]

---

[36] Your peace is not selfish. It is necessary.

Day 37: Overflowing with Compassion

Scripture:

"Clothe yourselves with compassion, kindness, humility, gentleness, and patience."
— *Colossians 3:12 (NIV)*

* * *

Affirmation:

I lead with compassion, including toward myself.

Reflection Prompt:

Where do you need more compassion right now, toward yourself or someone else?
What would it look like to respond gently instead of reacting quickly?

Journal Space:

Reflect & Respond

[37]

---

[37] Compassion begins when you stop judging your own healing process.

Day 38: Love That Builds, Not Breaks

Scripture:

"Encourage one another and build each other up..."
— *1 Thessalonians 5:11 (NIV)*

* * *

Affirmation:

I welcome relationships that strengthen my life.

Reflection Prompt:

Who in your life builds you up emotionally and spiritually?
Where are you being called to step away from relationships that
tear you down?

Journal Space:

Reflect & Respond

[38]

Day 39: Releasing Emotional Weight

Scripture:

"Cast your burden on the Lord, and he will sustain you."
— *Psalms 55:22 (ESV)*

* * *

Affirmation:

I release what is heavy. I choose peace.

Reflection Prompt:

What emotional weight have you been carrying that is not yours
to hold?
What would it feel like to lay it down completely?

Journal Space:

Reflect & Respond

[39]

---

[39] Sometimes the body heals when the heart stops carrying too much.

Day 40: Safe Love Takes Time

Scripture:

"Love is patient..."
— *1 Corinthians 13:4 (NIV)*

* * *

Affirmation:

I allow love to unfold slowly. I do not rush healing.

Reflection Prompt:

Where in your life are you rushing something that needs time?
What would it look like to trust slow love and steady growth?

Journal Space:

Reflect & Respond

[40]

---

[40] You do not need to force connection. What is real will grow.

Day 41: Healing Through Truth

Scripture:

"The Lord detests lying lips, but he delights in people who are trustworthy."
— *Proverbs 12:22 (NIV)*

* * *

Affirmation:

Truth strengthens me. Honesty protects my heart.

Reflection Prompt:

Where are you being invited to speak more honestly, with yourself or someone else?
What truth have you been avoiding because it feels uncomfortable?

Journal Space:

Reflect & Respond

[41]

---

[41] Truth may feel difficult at first, but it always brings clarity.

Day 42: Love as Medicine

Scripture:

"A cheerful heart is good medicine..."
— *Proverbs 17:22 (NIV)*

* * *

Affirmation:

Joy and love restore me. I allow goodness to enter my life.

Reflection Prompt:

What brings you genuine joy, not performance-based happiness?
Where could you invite more laughter, lightness, or love into your healing journey?

Journal Space:

Reflect & Respond

42

---

[42] Today, let yourself enjoy something simple without overthinking it.

Week 6 Reflection: Loving with Wisdom

Scripture:

"Above all, love each other deeply…"
— *1 Peter 4:8 (NIV)*

* * *

Affirmation:

I am learning that healthy love is steady, honest, and life-giving. Love is rooted in truth, compassion, and healthy boundaries.

Reflection Prompts:

This week invited you to explore love in a deeper way.

You practiced compassion toward yourself and discovered how softness can reach places that force never could.

1. Where did you notice growth in the way you protect your peace?
2. What relationship or dynamic feels clearer to you now than it did before?
3. Where are you being called to speak truth more gently and honestly?
4. What emotional weight have you released, even slightly?
5. What does safe, steady love look like for you moving forward?

Reflect & Respond

Day 43: Trusting Slow Growth

Scripture:

"Let perseverance finish its work so that you may be mature and complete, not lacking anything."
— *James 1:4 (NIV)*

* * *

Affirmation:

I trust the pace of my healing. I am becoming whole in time.

Reflection Prompt:

Where in your emotional life are you tempted to rush growth? What would it look like to trust the process instead of forcing it?

Journal Space:

Reflect & Respond

⁴³

Day 44: Strength in Vulnerability

Scripture:

"Trust in him at all times, you people; pour out your hearts to him, for God is our refuge."
— *Psalm 62:8 (NIV)*

* * *

Affirmation:

I heal and grow as I am honest about what I feel.

Reflection Prompt:

Where have you been pretending to be stronger than you feel?
Who feels safe enough for you to be emotionally honest with?

Journal Space:

Reflect & Respond

[44]

---

[44] Vulnerability shared with safe people builds connection.

Day 45: Releasing the Need to Control

Scripture:

"Trust in the Lord with all your heart and lean not on your own understanding."
— *Proverbs 3:5 (NIV)*

* * *

Affirmation:

I release control. I choose trust.

Reflection Prompt:

What situation are you trying to manage or control emotionally? What might shift if you surrendered the outcome to God?

Journal Space:

Reflect & Respond

---

[45] Control tightens the body. Trust allows it to soften.

Day 46: Love That Reflects God

Scripture:

"Dear friends, since God so loved us, we also ought to love one another."
— *1 John 4:11 (NIV)*

* * *

Affirmation:

I give and receive love in a way that reflects God's heart.

Reflection Prompt:

Does the love you are experiencing reflect patience, kindness, and truth?
Where might God be inviting you to love differently?

Journal Space:

Reflect & Respond

---

[46] Healthy love feels steady and safe.

Day 47: Emotional Discernment

Scripture:

"The wisdom from above is first pure; then peace-loving, considerate, submissive, full of mercy and good fruit..."
— *James 3:17 (NIV)*

* * *

Affirmation:

I am growing in wisdom. I trust what feels peaceful.

Reflection Prompt:

What decision or relationship currently feels confusing?
When you imagine the peaceful choice, what does it look like?

Journal Space:

Reflect & Respond

47

---

[47] Confusion is often a signal. Peace is a guide.

Day 48: Compassion Without Self-Abandonment

Scripture:

"Love your neighbor as yourself."
— *Mark 12:31 (NIV)*

* * *

Affirmation:

I care for others without neglecting myself.

Reflection Prompt:

Where have you prioritized others at the expense of your own well-being?
What would balanced compassion look like for you now?

Journal Space:

Reflect & Respond

[48]

---

[48] You are included in the need for love.

Day 49: Peace as Confirmation

Scripture:

"Let the peace of Christ rule in your hearts..."
— *Colossians 3:15 (NIV)*

* * *

Affirmation:

Peace confirms what is right for me.

Reflection Prompt:

Where have you felt peace recently, even in a difficult conversation?
What does your body tell you when something is aligned?

Journal Space:

Reflect & Respond

[49]

---

49 Peace is powerful clarity...

Week 7 Reflection: Discernment and Peace

Scripture:

"Peace I leave with you; my peace I give to you. Not as the world gives do I give to you. Let not your hearts be troubled, neither let them be afraid."
—*John 14:27 (NIV)*

* * *

Affirmation:

I trust the peace God places in my heart. It guides me with clarity.

Reflection Prompts:

This week invited you to deepen your emotional awareness.

You reflected on vulnerability, surrender, wisdom, and the quiet strength of letting go of control.

You began to notice the difference between intensity and peace.

1. Where did you practice vulnerability in a healthy way this week?
2. What situation required you to release control and choose trust instead?
3. Where did you feel a sense of peace that surprised you?
4. Which relationship feels more aligned with your values now?

Reflect & Respond

Day 50: Secure in Who I Am

Scripture:

"So in Christ Jesus you are all children of God through faith."
— *Galatians 3:26 (NIV)*

* * *

Affirmation:

My identity is secure. I do not have to earn love.

Reflection Prompt:

Where have you been seeking validation from others?
What would change if you fully believed you are already secure
in God?

Journal Space:

Reflect & Respond

⁵⁰

---

[50] Security allows your heart to relax. Allow that freedom.

Day 51: Loving Without Losing Yourself

Scripture:

"Stand firm then, with the belt of truth buckled around your
waist..."
— *Ephesians 6:14 (NIV)*

* * *

Affirmation:

I remain grounded in truth while loving others.

Reflection Prompt:

Have you ever shaped yourself to be more lovable?
What would it look like to stay fully yourself in your
relationships?

Journal Space:

Reflect & Respond

⁵¹

---

⁵¹ The "right" love does not require you to shrink.

Day 52: The Courage to Be Seen

Scripture:

"You are the light of the world."
— *Matthew 5:14 (NIV)*

* * *

Affirmation:

I am allowed to be seen as I am.

Reflection Prompt:

What parts of yourself do you tend to hide?
Who feels safe enough to let them see the real you?

Journal Space:

Reflect & Respond

[52]

---

[52] Being seen is part of being healed.

Day 53: Peace Over Performance

Scripture:

"Am I now trying to win the approval of human beings, or of God?"
— *Galatians 1:10 (NIV)*

* * *

Affirmation:

I choose peace over performance.

Reflection Prompt:

Where are you still performing instead of simply being?
What would it feel like to stop proving and start resting?

Journal Space:

Reflect & Respond

[53]

---

53 You do not have to impress to be loved. Be yourself!

Day 54: Healthy Detachment

Scripture:

"The Lord will fight for you; you need only to be still."
— *Exodus 14:14 (NIV)*

* * *

Affirmation:

I release what is not mine to carry.

Reflection Prompt:

What emotional responsibility are you holding that does not
belong to you?
What might happen if you gently handed it back?

Journal Space:

Reflect & Respond

54

---

54 Detachment is not indifference. It is clarity.

Day 55: Love Rooted in Freedom

Scripture:

"It is for freedom that Christ has set us free."
— *Galatians 5:1 (NIV)*

* * *

Affirmation:

Healthy love gives freedom.

Reflection Prompt:

Does your current love situation feel freeing or restricting?
What would freedom in love look like for you?

Journal Space:

Reflect & Respond

---

[55] Freedom is a sign of emotional safety.

Day 56: Overflow from Wholeness

Scripture:

"A good person brings good things out of the good stored up in their heart..."
— *Luke 6:45 (NIV)*

* * *

Affirmation:

I love from wholeness rather than neediness.

Reflection Prompt:

Are you loving from fullness or from a need to be filled?
What helps you return to emotional wholeness before giving again?

Journal Space:

Reflect & Respond

[56]

---

56 Overflow happens naturally when you are well.

Week 8 Reflection: Loving from Wholeness

Scripture:

"There is no fear in love. But perfect love drives out fear..."
— *1 John 4:18 (NIV)*

* * *

Affirmation:

I am learning to love from fullness, not from fear.

Reflection Prompts:

This week invited you to examine your identity and the way you give and receive love.

You reflected on validation, performance, freedom, and emotional responsibility.

You began to notice the difference between loving to be filled and loving from wholeness.

1. Where have you felt more secure in your identity this week?
2. What pattern of performance are you beginning to release?
3. Where did you practice healthy detachment instead of over-performing?
4. What does freedom in love look like for you now?

Reflect & Respond

Day 57: Trusting Your Discernment

Scripture:

"The wisdom of the prudent is to give thought to their ways..."
— *Proverbs 14:8 (NIV)*

* * *

Affirmation:

I trust the wisdom God is growing within me.

Reflection Prompt:

What decisions have you recently made that honored
your peace?
What does your body feel like when something is aligned?

Journal Space:

Reflect & Respond

⁵⁷

---

[57] Discernment strengthens when you listen to it.

Day 58: Choosing Mutual Love

Scripture:

"Carry each other's burdens…"
— *Galatians 6:2 (NIV)*

* * *

Affirmation:

I choose relationships that feel mutual and life-giving.

Reflection Prompt:

Where are you experiencing mutual support in your life?
Where have you been giving without receiving in return? Is it
an act of generosity and service, or are you in a trap of
codependency?

Journal Space:

Reflect & Respond

⁵⁸

---

[58] Healthy love flows both ways.

Day 59: Emotional Stability

Scripture:

"You will keep in perfect peace those whose minds are steadfast..."
— *Isaiah 26:3 (NIV)*

* * *

Affirmation:

I am becoming emotionally steady and secure.

Reflection Prompt:

What emotional trigger has softened for you over time?
What practice has helped you respond instead of react?

Journal Space:

Reflect & Respond

[59]

---

[59] Stability grows quietly through repetition and trust.

Day 60: Overflowing with Confidence

Scripture:

"May the God of hope fill you with all joy and peace as you trust in him..."
— *Romans 15:13 (NIV)*

* * *

Affirmation:

I am confident in the love I give and the love I receive.

Reflection Prompt:

What has shifted in your understanding of love over the past thirty days?
How do you feel different from when Part 2 began?

Journal Space:

Reflect & Respond

---

[60] Confidence in love grows when fear no longer leads.

Pause & Pray: Overflowing in Love

You have spent the last thirty days opening your heart
with wisdom.

You explored forgiveness.
You practiced boundaries.
You looked at patterns.
You learned the difference between intensity and peace.

That is growth.

Prayer:

God,

Thank you for teaching me that love does not have to hurt to
be real.

Help me continue to love from wholeness.
Help me trust my discernment.
Help me keep steady when emotions rise.

Heal what still feels sensitive in me.
Strengthen what is becoming secure.

Remind me that I do not have to chase love.
What is meant for me will meet me in peace.

As I move forward, let my heart remain open.

Let my love overflow and reflect Your patience and truth.

Amen.

Part 3: Thrive & Trust (Days 61–90)

"And the God of all grace...will himself restore you and make you strong, firm, and steadfast."
— *1 Peter 5:10 (NIV)*

You have replenished.

You have opened.

Now you begin to thrive!

This final section is about living from what has been restored, trusting the steadiness God is building within you.

Thriving does not mean perfection...
It means stability.
It means confidence rooted in identity, not approval.

In this season, you will reflect on resilience, purpose, gratitude, and the quiet strength of trust.

You are no longer just surviving.

You are becoming steady.
You are becoming strong.
You are becoming free.

Let's keep going!

* * *

Day 61: Strong and Steady

Scripture:

"Be strong and courageous. Do not be afraid...for the Lord your God goes with you."
— *Joshua 1:9 (NIV)*

* * *

Affirmation:

I am steady. I am supported. I am not alone.

Reflection Prompt:

Where in your life are you being called to stand more confidently?
Which fear is no longer leading you the way it once did?

Journal Space:

Reflect & Respond

61

---

61 Confidence grows when you remember He walks with you.

Day 62: Rooted Identity

Scripture:

"See what great love the Father has lavished on us, that we should be called children of God."
— *1 John 3:1 (NIV)*

* * *

Affirmation:

My identity is secure. I do not have to prove my worth.

Reflection Prompt:

Where do you still feel tempted to prove yourself?
What would shift if you lived fully from a secure identity instead?

Journal Space:

Reflect & Respond

Day 63: Resilience Refined

Scripture:

"Not only so, but we also glory in our sufferings, because we know that suffering produces perseverance..."
— *Romans 5:3–4 (NIV)*

* * *

Affirmation:

My challenges have strengthened me. I trust what they have shaped.

Reflection Prompt:

How has a past hardship refined your strength?
What resilience do you now carry that you didn't before?

Journal Space:

Reflect & Respond

[63]

---

[63] You are stronger than the season that tested you.

Week 9 Reflection: Flourishing in Faith

Scripture:

"And the God of all grace…will himself restore you and make you strong, firm, and steadfast."
— *1 Peter 5:10 (NIV)*

* * *

Affirmation:

I am becoming steady, strong, and rooted in who I am.

Reflection Prompts:

This week invited you to step into the confidence that comes from having a secure identity.

You reflected on identity, resilience, and the courage to move forward without fear leading you.

1. Where have you noticed new confidence emerging within you?
2. How has a past hardship strengthened your character?
3. Which fear feels smaller now than it once did?
4. In what ways are you beginning to trust yourself more?
5. What does thriving mean to you at this stage of your journey?

Reflect & Respond

Day 64: Living with Intention

Scripture:

"Be very careful, then, how you live—not as unwise but as wise."
— *Ephesians 5:15 (NIV)*

* * *

Affirmation:

I live intentionally. I move with clarity and peace.

Reflection Prompt:

Which area of your life feels most aligned right now?
Where do you want to be more intentional moving forward?

Journal Space:

Reflect & Respond

---

[64] Clarity creates calm momentum. Keep going...

Day 65: Joy Without Apology

Scripture:

"This is the day that the Lord has made; let us rejoice and be glad in it."
— *Psalm 118:24 (NIV)*

* * *

Affirmation:

I allow myself to experience joy fully and freely.

Reflection Prompt:

When do you feel most alive and light?
Have you ever minimized your joy to make others comfortable?

Journal Space:

Reflect & Respond

[65]

---

65 Joy is not indulgent. It is strengthening.

Day 66: Trusting His Timing

Scripture:

"He has made everything beautiful in its time."
— *Ecclesiastes 3:11 (NIV)*

* * *

Affirmation:

I trust God's timing in my life.

Reflection Prompt:

Where are you tempted to rush ahead?
What would it look like to trust the unfolding instead?

Journal Space:

Reflect & Respond

[66]

---

[66] What is meant for you will not miss you.

Day 67: Thriving in Peace

Scripture:

"You will go out in joy and be led forth in peace..."
— *Isaiah 55:12 (NIV)*

* * *

Affirmation:

I thrive in peace. I walk forward with confidence.

Reflection Prompt:

What does thriving mean to you now, compared to earlier in
your journey?
Where do you feel the most peace in your life today?

Journal Space:

Reflect & Respond

[67]

Day 68: Confidence Without Comparison

Scripture:

"Each one should test their own actions...without comparing themselves to someone else."
— *Galatians 6:4 (NIV)*

* * *

Affirmation:

I celebrate my growth without comparison.

Reflection Prompt:

In what ways do you tend to compare yourself?
How does comparison affect your sense of peace?

Journal Space:

Reflect & Respond

Day 69: Strength with Softness

Scripture:

"Clothe yourselves with compassion, kindness, humility, gentleness, and patience."
— *Colossians 3:12 (NIV)*

* * *

Affirmation:

I am strong and gentle at the same time.

Reflection Prompt:

Where have you confused strength with hardness?
What would strong softness or gentle strength look like in your life right now?

Journal Space:

Reflect & Respond

---

[69] True strength does not require harshness.

Day 70: Purpose with Peace

Scripture:

"For we are God's handiwork, created in Christ Jesus to do good works..."
— *Ephesians 2:10 (NIV)*

* * *

Affirmation:

My life has purpose, and I walk in it peacefully.

Reflection Prompt:

What feels purposeful in your life right now?
How can you pursue purpose without pressure?

Journal Space:

Reflect & Respond

70

---

70 Purpose grows best in a peaceful heart.

Week 10 Reflection: Living with Calm Confidence

Scripture:

"For you make me glad by your deeds, Lord; I sing for joy at what your hands have done."
— *Psalm 92:4 (NIV)*

* * *

Affirmation:

I am learning to thrive with calm confidence and steady joy.

Reflection Prompts:

This week invited you to explore what thriving truly means—allowing yourself to experience the fullness of life.

Not comparing or proving yourself but gently living intentionally, joyfully, and peacefully.

1. Where are you living more intentionally than you once did?
2. What comparison are you ready to release for good?
3. How has your definition of strength changed?
4. Where are you experiencing joy without apology?
5. What does peaceful purpose look like in your daily life?

Reflect & Respond

Day 71: Calm Leadership

Scripture:

"The Lord gives strength to his people; the Lord blesses his people with peace."
— *Psalm 29:11 (NIV)*

* * *

Affirmation:

I lead my life with calm strength and steady peace.

Reflection Prompt:

Where are you being called to lead more confidently in your life? What does calm leadership look like for you personally?

Journal Space:

Reflect & Respond

[71]

---

[71] Leadership rooted in peace is powerful.

Day 72: Grounded and Unshaken

Scripture:

"Therefore, everyone who hears these words of mine and puts them into practice is like a wise man who built his house on the rock."
— *Matthew 7:24 (NIV)*

* * *

Affirmation:

I am grounded. I am not easily shaken.

Reflection Prompt:

What foundations have you strengthened in this season? What used to shake you that no longer does?

Journal Space:

Reflect & Respond

---

[72] Stability is built slowly and intentionally.

Day 73: Gratitude as Strength

Scripture:

"Give thanks to the Lord, for he is good; his love endures forever."
— *Psalm 107:1 (NIV)*

* * *

Affirmation:

Gratitude strengthens my heart and steadies my mind. I express gratitude for at least one thing each day.

Reflection Prompt:

What part of your journey are you most grateful for now? Which hardship did you gain strength from?

Journal Space:

Reflect & Respond

---

[73] Gratitude anchors you in your abundance.

Day 74: Confidence Without Arrogance

Scripture:

"Let another praise you, and not your own mouth…"
— *Proverbs 27:2 (NIV)*

* * *

Affirmation:

I walk confidently without needing validation.

Reflection Prompt:

Where do you feel solid in who you are?
Where are you still tempted to seek others' approval?

Journal Space:

Reflect & Respond

---

[74] True confidence might be quiet.

Day 75: Living Fully Awake

Scripture:

"Be alert and of sober mind. Your enemy the devil prowls around like a roaring lion looking for someone to devour."
— *1 Peter 5:8 (NIV)*

* * *

Affirmation:

I live awake, aware, and intentionally.

Reflection Prompt:

Where in your life do you feel most present right now?
What distraction are you ready to release?
Where are you being called to be more aware or intentional?

Journal Space:

Reflect & Respond

Day 76: Feminine Strength

Scripture:

"She is clothed with strength and dignity..."
— *Proverbs 31:25 (NIV)*

* * *

Affirmation:

I embody strength and dignity in how I live.

Reflection Prompt:

What does strength look like in your life today?
How has your understanding of feminine power evolved?

Journal Space:

Reflect & Respond

---

76 Dignity grows when you honor yourself. You matter.

Day 77: Trusting Your Future

Scripture:

"'For I know the plans I have for you,' declares the Lord, 'plans to prosper you and not to harm you, plans to give you hope and a future.'"
— *Jeremiah 29:11 (NIV)*

* * *

Affirmation:

My future is guided. I walk forward with trust, knowing He is with me.

Reflection Prompt:

What excites you about the next chapter of your life?
What fear about the future feels lighter than it once did?

Journal Space:

Reflect & Respond

⁷⁷

---

77 Trust makes the future feel spacious.

Week 11 Reflection: Steady and Awake

Scripture:

"She is clothed with strength and dignity; she can laugh at the days to come."
— *Proverbs 31:25 (NIV)*

* * *

Affirmation:

I walk forward steady, aware, and confident in who I am becoming.

Reflection Prompts:

This week you may have dug deeper into embodying your strength. With ease. Gentle, grounded, peaceful, and confident.

You reflected on gratitude, stability, feminine strength, and trust for the good in your future.

Take a few minutes to reflect:

1. Where have you stepped into leadership in your own life?
2. What foundation now feels solid within you?
3. How has gratitude shifted your perspective recently?
4. Which future hope feels clearer or lighter than before?
5. What does strength look like for you today compared to earlier in your journey?

Reflect & Respond

Day 78: Living Your Legacy

Scripture:

"The righteous lead blameless lives; blessed are their children after them."
— *Proverbs 20:7 (NIV)*

* * *

Affirmation:

I live in a way that reflects the strength I have built. Amen.
Read that again.

Reflection Prompt:

What kind of legacy are you building through your daily choices? Which values feel most important for you to develop now?

Journal Space:

Reflect & Respond

78

Day 79: Anchored in Faith

Scripture:

"We have this hope as an anchor for the soul, firm and secure."
— *Hebrews 6:19 (NIV)*

* * *

Affirmation:

My soul is at ease and anchored. I am steady in hope.

Reflection Prompt:

What anchors you when uncertainty rises?
How has your faith grown stronger through recent challenges?

Journal Space:

Reflect & Respond

---

[79] Anchored hearts stay in flow with peace.

Day 80: Integrated Strength

Scripture:

"I can do all this through him who gives me strength."
— *Philippians 4:13 (NIV)*

* * *

Affirmation:

My strength is integrated; each part of my life reflects this.

Reflection Prompt:

How are you stronger now than you were at the beginning of this journey?
Where does your strength feel calm rather than reactive?

Journal Space:

Reflect & Respond

---

[80] Integrated strength feels steady and whole.

Day 81: Humility in Leadership

Scripture:

"Whoever wants to become great among you must be your servant."
— *Matthew 20:26 (NIV)*

* * *

Affirmation:

I don't need to force my way to the front. I lead with integrity, humility, and clarity.

Reflection Prompt:

Where are you leading in quiet ways that matter?
How can you lead without losing your gentleness?

Journal Space:

Reflect & Respond

[81]

---

[81] True leadership reflects character and guides you.

Day 82: Emotional Maturity

Scripture:

"When I was a child, I talked like a child... When I became a man,
I put the ways of childhood behind me."
— *1 Corinthians 13:11 (NIV)*

* * *

Affirmation:

I respond with maturity and wisdom.

Reflection Prompt:

Which emotional reactions have you outgrown?
How do you handle conflict differently now?

Journal Space:

Reflect & Respond

---

82 Maturity shows in your response, not your reaction.

Day 83: Peaceful Ambition

Scripture:

"Commit to the Lord whatever you do, and he will establish your plans."
— *Proverbs 16:3 (NIV)*

* * *

Affirmation:

I pursue growth without losing peace.

Reflection Prompt:

What goal feels aligned with your values right now?
How can you pursue it without pressure or striving?

Journal Space:

Reflect & Respond

---

83 Ambition and peace can coexist. Go after it.

Day 84: Living Fully Aware

Scripture:

"So teach us to number our days, that we may gain a heart of wisdom."
— *Psalm 90:12 (NIV)*

* * *

Affirmation:

I live fully present and awake to my life.

Reflection Prompt:

What feels most meaningful in this season of your life? Where are you choosing awareness instead of coasting on autopilot?

Journal Space:

Reflect & Respond

[84]

---

[84] Consider going off "auto" mode in at least one area today.

Week 12 Reflection: Becoming Steady

Scripture:

"...He set my feet on a rock and gave me a firm place to stand."
— Psalm 40:2 (NIV)

* * *

Affirmation:

I am steady. I am restored. I trust who I have become. I'm excited to move forward!

Reflection Prompts:

This week invited you to step fully into integration.

Living awake, grounded, and anchored in who you are.

You reflected on legacy, leadership, maturity, peaceful ambition, and awareness. This is a full-circle moment!

1. Where do you feel the most integrated in your body, heart, and spirit?
2. Which part of your old self feels distant now?
3. How has your understanding of strength evolved over the past few months?
4. What kind of woman are you becoming?
5. What feels steady in you that once felt fragile?

Reflect & Respond

Day 85: Anchored in Wholeness

Scripture:

"The one who calls you is faithful, and he will do it."
— *1 Thessalonians 5:24 (NIV)*

* * *

Affirmation:

I am anchored in wholeness. I trust the work God is completing in me.

Reflection Prompt:

Where do you feel most whole right now? *Sit with this for a minute and feel the calm.*
Which part of your healing no longer feels fragile?

Journal Space:

Reflect & Respond

[85]

---

[85] Consider talking about your wholeness with others. Share
the goodness!

Day 86: Living Without Fear

Scripture:

"For God has not given us a spirit of fear, but of power, love, and a sound mind."
— *2 Timothy 1:7 (NIV)*

* * *

Affirmation:

Fear is behind me. I move forward in clarity and strength.

Reflection Prompt:

Which former fear has lost its grip on you?
Where are you stepping forward more confidently than before?

Journal Space:

Reflect & Respond

[86]

---

[86] Courage often feels both calming and exciting!

Day 87: Peace as Your Foundation

Scripture:

"Great peace have those who love your law, and nothing can make them stumble."
— *Psalm 119:165 (NIV)*

* * *

Affirmation:

Peace is my foundation; it nourishes my soul. I am not easily agitated.

Reflection Prompt:

What used to unsettle you that no longer does?
What daily practice now protects your peace?

Journal Space:

Reflect & Respond

[87]

---

[87] Peace is built through small moments and faithful choices.

Day 88: Fully Alive

Scripture:

"I have come that they may have life and have it to the full."
— *John 10:10 (NIV)*

* * *

Affirmation:

I allow myself to live life fully and freely.

Reflection Prompt:

Where do you feel most alive in this moment?
What are you no longer willing to settle for?

Journal Space:

Reflect & Respond

---

88 Living fully begins with honoring what matters most.

Day 89: Trusting the Road Ahead

Scripture:

"The Lord will guide you always..."
— *Isaiah 58:11 (NIV)*

* * *

Affirmation:

I trust the road ahead. I am guided and supported. He is my guiding light.

Reflection Prompt:

What future hope feels clearer than it once did?
What are you ready to walk toward without hesitation?
Feel free to choose it.

Journal Space:

Reflect & Respond

[89]

---

[89] Guidance unfolds one faithful step at a time.

Day 90: Watered and Whole

Scripture:

"He refreshes my soul."
— *Psalm 23:3 (NIV)*

Amen.

* * *

Affirmation:

I am watered. The woman I have become is nourished and whole.

Reflection Prompt:

How would you have described yourself when you began this journey?
How do you describe yourself now?

Journal Space:

Reflect & Respond

---

[90] You did not rush this. You became it. You are a gift to those around you.

Final Reflection: Looking Back, Moving Forward

Scripture:

"Forget the former things; do not dwell on the past. See, I am doing a new thing!"
— *Isaiah 43:18–19 (NIV)*

* * *

Affirmation:

I embrace all that has been done within me and trust the growth that will continue.

Reflection Prompts:

You have completed ninety days.
Let that sink in.
Look back at your first entries.
Notice the tone, fears, questions, reactions.
Now notice the steadiness in your words today.

1. What has shifted most in you during this journey?
2. Which daily rhythm do you want to carry forward?
3. Which boundary feels stronger now?
4. What truth about yourself do you believe more deeply?
5. What season are you stepping into next?

Reflect & Respond

Pause & Pray

You have walked through ninety days of reflection, honesty, and growth. Breathe.

You have faced what needed healing.
You have softened what you once guarded.
You have strengthened what once felt fragile.

Be proud.

Prayer:

God,

Thank you for walking with me through this season.

Help me remember that nourishment is not a phase;
it is an everyday practice.

Keep my heart open and anchored.

Keep my body steady and supported.

Keep my mind clear and grounded in truth.

And when I forget, gently remind me:

I am watered.
I am whole.
And I am becoming.

Amen.

Conclusion

"Being confident of this, that he who began a good work in you
will carry it on to completion..."
— *Philippians 1:6 (NIV)*

* * *

Healing is layered.

Likely you will revisit some of these themes again. You may
encounter new seasons that stretch you in different ways.

You'll always have this book, your work, as a reminder you are
more powerful than you thought.

This journal was never meant to be a finish line. Rather, it's a
remembrance of this season, this part of your journey.

A reminder that nourishment matters.
    That love must be healthy to be holy.
    That strength can be gentle.
    That peace is more powerful than noise.

Return to these pages whenever you need grounding.

Wholeness is not something you chase. It is something you
practice and embody.

— Jackie

About the Author

Jackie Frary is a wellness advocate, functional health coach, and author who believes healing begins when the mind, body, and spirit are brought back into alignment.

After years of navigating mystery symptoms and fatigue, Jackie became the CEO of her own healing, integrating functional medicine principles with faith-centered mindfulness, nourishment, and grounded lifestyle practices.

She is the author of *The Internal Fungus Among Us* and the founder of Forward ThinKer Wellness and Forward ThinKer Press, where she develops educational resources and devotional tools designed to support restoration, resilience, and purposeful living.

Jackie holds certifications in Nutrition, Life and Wellness Coaching, Ayurveda, and body-based therapeutic practices. Her work bridges practical health strategy with spiritual integration, empowering others to rebuild from depletion into steadiness.

When she is not writing or collaborating with wellness and faith communities, Jackie can be found hiking, journaling in quiet coffee shops, or teaching others how to listen to the wisdom of their own bodies.

Her *From Soil to Soul™ Devotional* series continues to grow, with future volumes exploring blooming, belonging, grief, refinement, and the faithful unfolding of each season of life.

www.forwardthinkerwellness.com
Facebook: ForwardThinKerWellness
Instagram: @jackieftwellness

Also by Jackie Frary

From Soil to Soul™: Rooted & Renewed
A 90-Day Devotional Journal of Healing Scriptures, Reflections & Whole-Body Renewal
Forward ThinKer Press, 2025

Explore the full *From Soil to Soul™ Devotional* series at www.forwardthinkerwellness.com

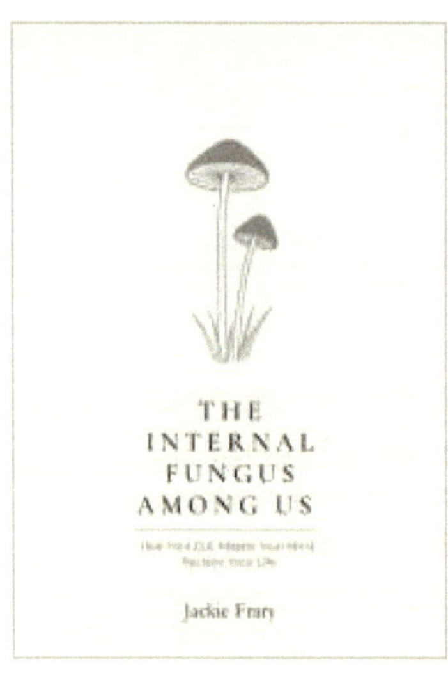

The Internal Fungus Among Us
A Functional and Faith-Centered Journey to Heal the Gut-Brain Connection and Renew Your Energy
Forward ThinKer Press, 2025